Craft Fayre Success

A Guide to Choosing Craft Fayres

Angela Edwards

Edition 1 - 2016

ISBN-13:978-1532737084

DEDICATION

Daniel: the reason my heart beats, my eyes light up and my life
is filled with joy.

ACKNOWLEDGMENT

Life is a journey and we don't travel alone. This book has been made possible due to all the people who has touched my life, from family and friends, teachers, colleagues, craft fair organisers, stall holders, customers and clients.

Everyone has taught me something, consciously or unconsciously. We all have something to learn and all have something to share. Every experience, good or bad has brought me to this point in my life today. Every day I am grateful for life's experiences big or small, positive or negative. I try to find the learning in everything, sometimes it is easy to find, other times its difficult.

I am grateful for all my experiences on this life journey.

CONTENTS

FORMS

INTRODUCTION

Starting a business is a dream and goal held by many people and now it is easier than ever to start making money by selling items you have enjoyed making. There has never been a better time to start a creative business, working for yourself and being the boss!

Many people start out on a casual basis, doing a few craft fayres at weekends and bank holidays, fitting in around family and work whilst others get involved on a more regular basis, some even running their venture on a part or full time basis.

People have many reasons for starting their venture including:

- Selling designs and work that has been made as part a hobby

- Earning extra money to supplement the family income

- Building up a pot of money to add to their pension funds

- Generating funds to pay for a holiday, special occasion or luxury item

- Growing a long term business with the view of providing an escape plan from the day job they no longer enjoy

Whatever you reasons, there is plenty of room and opportunities to fulfil your goals.

The craft industry has seen huge growth in recent years as people book stalls at craft fayres to sell their handmade work. To support the needs of this community, there has been an increase in businesses organising craft fayres of different types, sizes and descriptions, providing a valuable service to crafters, designers and makers. Each week there are numerous opportunities across the country to attend fayres in order to meet customers, sell your wares and grow your business. With the increase of craft fayres available, it can be a minefield deciding which type of event is right for you. Choose the wrong event, and it can be expensive and unrewarding, but select the right ones and it can be fulfilling, exciting and satisfying as you see your business grow.

Who is This Book For?

This book is for you if:

- You are thinking about selling your work at craft fayres

- You have tried a few craft fayres and not had the results you wanted and deserved

- You want to find craft fayres that work for you

- You can only do a few craft fayres each year and want to find quality events

- You need to know how to prepare for craft fayres so you can maximise your chances of success.

Written in an easy to follow and practical format with forms at the back that you can use, this book is based on my experience of finding and attending craft fayres to grow my business.

Over the years, I learnt the value of taking time to carefully research, plan and prepare for each event in order to maximise every opportunity. In the early days of doing craft fayres, I chose events at random, mainly based on price and the closest to home and found this method very hit and miss. I learnt from every event I attended and in time, realized that the key to success was in the research and careful selection in choosing the right events for me and my products and also in the planning and preparation. I learnt from every event, both the good and bad, successful and unsuccessful, the highs and lows and now I share my experience and teach others via coaching and training programmes how to avoid costly errors and get the best out of every craft fayre.

Amongst all the joys and disappointments, I learnt that enjoying the event was important as attending craft fayres can be hard work and involve long days, but finding the opportunities to make friends (both other traders and customers), being comfortable on the day and having fun was essential. There were some occasions when the event didn't bring in the results that I expected, but I thoroughly enjoyed myself and was glad I attended – if nothing else for a good day out.

I hope you find this book of value. There are no quick fixes or guarantees of anything, but if you can learn from my experience and feel confident in choosing and attending future craft fayres, then writing this book will have been worth it.

I wish you every success.

3

ABOUT THE AUTHOR

As far back as I can remember, I enjoyed crafting. One of my earliest memories is being about 4 years old and winding the bobbing with cotton ready for my mother to use in her sewing machine. As I got older, my mother taught me to pin the pattern to the fabric, insert tailor tacks, cut out the pattern and eventually sew garments together. I loved it. By the time I reached secondary school at the age of 11, I was skilled at dressmaking for my age, so my teacher gave me additional projects such as making bags and soft toys. I loved sewing and spent many hours reading dressmaking and sewing magazines and collecting patterns and fabrics. I dreamed of writing a book to inspire others about my passion.

A few years later when I started my career in Human Resource Management, I realized I can achieve whatever I wanted, as long as I was prepared to work hard. With this realisation, I set about deciding what I wanted, planned and worked towards achieving it. I soon found myself achieving many things in my life and career including creating my ideal job, coaching and training others to start a creative business.

I have been on the same journey as you – that of indulging in making beautiful craft items (including jewellery, candles, cards, textile goods and soft furnishings) and exploring different avenues to sell my work. I am now making embarking on a new dream of being an author, sharing my knowledge and experience with the vision of inspiring someone.

Who am I? I am Angela Edwards, mother to an amazing young man and a gorgeous dependent cat! For over 30 years, I worked with Private, Public, Charitable and Voluntary Sector Organisations specialising in people management, training and development. I gained professional qualifications for my field and progressed to managing Training and Human Resource Departments working at senior and director level. As part of my roles, I worked with people at all levels, helping to develop skills, impart knowledge and ultimately develop confidence so they could deliver effective, efficient and profitable products and services.

In recent years, I carved a career in the Craft Industry, running my own business. I have done craft fayres of all types, sizes and descriptions and learnt an enormous amount along the way. This book is an outpouring of many things I learnt whilst looking for craft fayres to sell my work. It documents many of my learning and experiences along the way – both good and not so good.

These days I am focused on helping people who want to start a creative business by offering a range of services through the Jewellery & Crafts Academy. With my professional corporate background and the experience of running my own creative business, I have the privilege helping others get started and become profitable quicker than if they were working on their own.

This book is based on my own real experiences which I have had the opportunity to share with hundreds of people on various training courses. I have been blessed with helping people turn their hobby into a business and watching them achieve their dreams and change their lives. I hope that by reading this book, it will make a difference to you and your business.

Angela Edwards

CRAFT FAYRES
THIS WAY!

1.0   Type of Craft Fayres

In recent years, the craft industry has seen huge growth providing opportunities for crafters, designers and makers to start a business and sell their work. Each week, there are hundreds of opportunities available across the country to attend fayres of varying sizes and types. Understanding the type of craft fayres available and the kind of customers it attracts can help you decide whether an event is right for you and your products. Craft Fayres can include:

School Fayres

These events are a regular occurrence in many schools, particularly around Christmas, Easter and towards the end of term in the summer. Often organised by the PTA (Parent Teacher Association), these events are organised to raise funds for the school. Children and parents will usually have stalls, and businesses in the local community are often encouraged to set up also. It is usual for a small fee to be charged.

School craft fayres usually attract not only children, parents and teachers, but the local community who want to support the school. Advertising for the event is often limited and done mainly through providing children with newsletters and details of the event to take home to parents, family and friends. There may also be adverts in local newspapers, shop windows and via any social media pages that the school may run. Depending on the size and location of the school, turnout can be varied.

9

As the events are local, with mainly children attending, and adults there to support the school, do pay attention to the type of products and prices you offer. Small ticket items, costing a few pounds will often go well. There may be opportunities to talk to teachers and other adults attending, so do be prepared with marketing information explaining your main style of work and more wider ranges on offer so you can generate interest and sales at a later date.

Community Events

Community events are often held in Village Halls, Church Halls and Community Centres and organised by a committee. Do be aware that sometimes, private individuals hire the venue and organise their own private craft fayre events which can be independent of the venue committee.

When organised by the committee, it is often as part of a fundraising programme. The whole village, church members and community will be invited and encouraged to be involved – these are usually promoted as fun days, festivals, carnivals etc. The event will often be advertised by the local community and sometimes local businesses will have flyers and posters in their windows to advertise the event. There may be articles in the local newspaper promoting and encouraging people to attend. These can be good events with high footfall and lots of trade. If they are held outdoors, attendance can be weather dependant.

There will be local advertising with these events it may extend to posters and street signs, social media marketing and leaflet drops. The methods of marketing and advertising will vary. There will usually be a fee for stalls and prices will vary.

Private Businesses – when events are organised by private individuals, it is usually done for profit. These events can be just as well organised and successful. If you are keen to support the fundraising efforts of the village hall, church or community centre, do check that and make sure you know who you will be trading with.

Charity Events
Charities often advertise fundraising events to raise funds for their cause and to raise awareness. Many charities will often support a wide variety of craft stalls at their fundraising event. As charities often have lots of supporters, it is not unusual for them to advertise and market the event directly via community fundraisers. People who want to support the charity will often attend, and these events can be very popular and provide good trading opportunities.

Charity events can range enormously, from a typical small craft fayre in church halls with standard table top set up to a glamourous gala evening professionally organised with luxury shopping area. Do explore the type of event you wish to book as this will determine your products and prices, for example, if your event is being held in a church hall, the products and prices being sought are likely to be small ticket items compared a gala evening event which may see people prepared to spend more for luxury pieces.

Some organisers may ask for a donation of one or more product to be entered as a raffle prize. This can offer a good marketing opportunity, so do ensure your products are well labelled with your business name, website and other contact details so the winner of the prize can contact you again in future.

Artisan Markets

Artisan craft fayre and markets are available but opportunity may be limited to find across the country. Where these exist, organisers often operate a strict criteria with regards to what they will accept as "Artisan" and will often expect items to be made from high quality materials and be finished to exacting standards.

Products and prices need to be reflective of the high standards of the markets. People who seek out and visit Artisan markets and fayres will generally be looking for specialist one off pieces and often prepared to pay handsomely for quality pieces. Do think about building a brand as an artisan designer, as many lovers of artisan work often seek to build a collection of over time.

General Gift and Craft Fayres

These types of fayres are most popular and are widely organised across the country. They will all vary with some organisers accepting a mixture of mass produced goods and handcrafted items in varying degrees. Fayres of this type can range from small local events costing a few pounds right up to large national, multi day operations costing thousands.

At these type of events, there will often be lots of competition within the same category of products, i.e. Jewellery, Candles, Bags etc, so explore with the organiser whether they will be any limits on the number of other traders who will be selling the same type of products as yourself. Some organisers operate a policy of having a limit of 2 traders selling the same type of products at their event.

Held across the country, general gift and craft fayres are popular with traders. Some events may be held on an annual, monthly or weekly basis, whilst others may be just one off events. When well organised, and in the right location, these events can provide regular trading opportunities.

County Shows

For many years, large scale county shows have been very popular. Held across the UK mainly from April to October, they are operated within large showgrounds, country parks and the grounds of prestigious country manors.

These events attract a wide range of businesses including the farming and agricultural community, high end designer outlets, upcoming brands, high street brands and handcrafted business owners. Attracting thousands of exhibitors ready to showcase and sell their wares they can also draw hundreds of thousands of visitors and shoppers over several days.

At these events, businesses can either rent space directly with the organiser or their agent by the square metre. Exhibitors will often be required to provide their own gazebo and equipment including a generator for electricity, as all that is provided by the organiser is the outdoor space. This will vary so do check. Creativity is required to ensure an attractive sales area within your gazebo. This option can start from a several hundred pounds for a standard 3 x 3 metre space (standard size of a gazebo).

It is usual for event management companies to offer space within their large shopping marquee. Several independent companies set up specifically to provide opportunities to small traders to showcase and sell their work. This can be a good idea to trade with them as you will receive the benefit of being under a large shopping marquee that has been organised and run to support the craft community and small traders, plus, the cost of having a trading space is much more affordable than renting space with the showground organiser or agent.

Being positioned with other traders of a similar size and background enables you to make friends and support each other over the duration of the event. Space is often allocated by the square metre and you are responsible for setting up your space with any suitable display equipment. Creativity is required to ensure an attractive sales area. This option can start from a few hundred pounds for a 2 x 1 metre space.

A wide range of shoppers from all backgrounds and from around the country attend these events and therefore can provide good trading opportunities for all types of traders.

Cultural Carnivals and Music Festivals

These types of events can attract visitors from all over the country and the world due to their popularity, extensive marketing and celebrity headline acts. They can attract hundreds of thousands of visitors each year and can last for several days.

Such events can be held in a variety of outdoor venues ranging from designated streets within the inner cities to private farm or council parks. Designed to bring the whole community together, they can be very well attended and hugely popular. Whilst many of the events are designed to attract families, some of the very large music festivals may have age restrictions and children may not be allowed.

Many organisers require traders to complete an application form and a strict criteria may apply. Application may need to be submitted many months in advance, so do check the website of any events you are interested in attending. If your application is successful, a deposit may be required to secure the booking. Some events can run in to many hundreds if not thousands of pounds for a small pitch and you may be required to provide your own gazebo and equipment. Caravan Parks and camp sites are sometimes provided for a small fee, enabling traders to stay near the site overnight.

Council Craft Fayres, Food Markets and Christmas Events
Many Councils will organise events throughout the year such as handmade craft fayres, specialty food markets, business shows and Christmas shopping markets. These are often organised by the Events team in departments such as Economic Regeneration or Leisure and Recreation.

It may be worth contacting your local council and exploring events they organise and getting on their list of traders, so when plans are being made and traders are being sought, you can be contacted. Many councils will require traders to have insurance of up to £5million cover, so do check with them in advance and ensure you have appropriate level of cover. Trading standards are often present at these events too, so do ensure all your goods and business meet their standards.

Themed Fayres

Each year there are many themed events available across the country including Health, Beauty, Holistic, Spiritual, Gardening, Flowers, Vintage, Cars, Trains, Books, Food, Pets, History etc. These events attract enthusiasts, hobbyists and people generally interested in these areas and items closely related. Many organisers will often welcome creative businesses to trade if their products are likely to be of interest to their members or visitors. Many of these specialist areas will have formed a national society, association or membership site so if your products fit within a niche area, then do consider contacting them for details of forthcoming events.

Shopping Centres

Craft fayres and craft markets held in shopping centres have become popular in the past few years as the management find new ways of attracting the public back in to the area as shops have closed. Opportunities will vary from area to area, but it's worth checking with either the local council for markets or the shopping centre management team. Events can be organised by either the shopping centre management or an events management company appointed by the council or shopping centre. If held in a busy area, they can be present regular trading opportunities.

These are a selection of different craft fayres available and this list is not exhaustive.

SEEK AND YOU WILL FIND!

2.0 Finding Craft Fayres

Each week, there are thousands of craft fayres happening across the country in local communities. Finding them can be easy if you know where to look. Places include:

- Local newspapers and community magazines
  Do check news articles as church groups, community centres, village halls and charities sometimes have a news item promoting their event.

- Internet searches
  There are several companies set up online to provide event organisers with opportunities to list their events and traders to find them. Doing internet searches for craft fayres in your area can bring them up.

- Local supermarket notice boards and shop windows
  Many event organisers of small local community events will often advertise here. Also check the notice boards of post offices.

- Community Centres, Village, Church Halls and Schools
  As these are popular places for small local events to be held, do check in with admin staff regularly.

- Networking and Crafting Social Media Groups

  There may be social media groups set up for your craft specialism online, so do check with group users for any forthcoming events they may know of. Many people are willing to share information.

- Local Council Events Team

  Many councils will have a team that organise markets and events, particularly in the run up to Christmas. Do check with them and register your details so you can be notified when they are opening up places for booking.

- Large Specialist Shows

  Do check the website of national or regional exhibition venues as they will often promote events and have a link to the event organiser. Also, do check any special interest magazines or websites as they will often list details of any regular shows they are organising or involved with.

- County Shows

  Listen to your local news and conduct internet searches for any showgrounds in your area. The website of showgrounds will often promote events throughout the year. In addition, they often run radio or TV adverts a few weeks before the event.

- Word of Mouth

  Keeping in touch with event organisers, asking them where they advertise, and also to put you on their mailing list so they can send you details of their future events can be useful. Also do talk to other traders and ask them who they trade with as they can provide valuable insight and put you in touch with other organisers.

Do always look and listen out for opportunities as they are all around. It is more usual to find more craft fayre opportunities from March to August (over the spring and summer period) and again from October to December (in the run up to Christmas). The months of January and February are usually the slowest for events, but organisers may still operate a few, particularly if the venue is near shopping centres that are holding sales events or are charity focused.

LOCAL TARGET!

3.0 Local Events

Starting and growing your business locally is very important. People and communities like to support local businesses for a variety of reasons including:

* Building rapport with local people
* Establishing business relationships with the local community
* Supporting the local economy
* Reduced carbon emissions
* Contributing to saving the environment

Over time, when you are trading in regular outlets in your community, people will get to know you and your business. You will be building trust. People like to know that a business is going to be around – that they are not "here today, gone tomorrow". It can take time to build this trust, but it will come, and when people trust you, they will support you and your business.

A few years ago I was attending a craft fayre in my local area about 4 weeks before Christmas. I was set up next to a lady named Patricia who had a wonderful product which was beautifully displayed. In addition, she had a great sales pitch. I got talking with Patricia throughout the day, and at the end of the event she expressed how disappointed she was.

I was surprised as the event was very busy with a good flow of customers, and I noticed she was selling lots of products. Patricia explained that she had taken far less money than she had expected. She went on to explain that with a few weeks before Christmas, she expected to take between £700 for the day and had only taken £125.

As the conversation progressed, she explained that she didn't live in the area and travelled about 2 hours to get the event (a total of 4 hours round trip) She had heard from a friend that the area was "affluent" and people attended craft fayres, making purchases at this prestigious venue and that was her reason for attending. Patricia then went on to express that she had been running her business for over 6 years and had built up a regular customer base in her local area.

Over the years, she networked regularly with other local businesses, worked with many of the local colleges and schools teaching her craft, supported lots of community fundraising events plus attended 2 regular markets each month in her local town. With all this hard work, she had built a regular and loyal customer base who purchased from her regularly as the students, parents, teachers, local business owners and the general community knew her. Therefore on a regular market day, it was normal for her to take several hundreds of pounds and a few weeks before Christmas it was usual to double and or triple her normal takings per day.

I met Patricia at the Craft Fayre on Sunday and she explained that she had taken about £800 the day before in her local area and coming to the craft fayre at this prestigious venue was expecting about £700 in takings.

During the conversation, it dawned on me that the reason her expectations wasn't realized was nothing to do with her product, sales pitch, venue or location, but rather it was because no-one knew her. Patricia was outside of her area and had no connections. People had not seen her or heard of her before – they didn't know her business name, didn't know the quality of her product and therefore there was no trust.

This is a classic example why building locally, makes good business sense. Sometimes we feel the "grass is greener" elsewhere and we spend time, money and energy travelling the country to events in the belief that "this is where the money is" only to be disappointed – I have done this myself on many occasions, only to discover that any takings barely covered my travel, accommodation, subsistence and time, resulting in a loss. When I started focusing on doing local events, building up my name and reputation, I started to see a difference in my profits!

KEEP IN TOUCH!

4.0 Using Mailing Lists

Building mailing lists can be a valuable tool to use in your business. It is not uncommon for new and established businesses to purchase mailing lists from data gathering and marketing companies. These lists can be very expensive, running into hundreds of pounds.

Building your own list costs nothing and is quick and easy to do, with the added advantage that you have met the person and have a level of rapport with them. Craft fayres can provide an excellent opportunity to gather contact details for your mailing list (See Form 1 in the Forms Section at the back of this book). This simple task can help your business to grow online if you choose to sell your work this way too.

Contact details can be collected in several ways including:

- Running a competition on your stall
- Inviting people to enter your Free Prize Draw

These are easy to set up and can be fun. Alternatively, the easiest way is to ask people if they would like to join your mailing list and receive updates of special offers. In my experience, around 90% of people I have asked have been willing to provide their details and I write their name and email address on my list.

In the past when I have asked people to write their details down, sometimes it was hard to read the writing and so I lost some contacts. I quickly learnt that it was easier to write it down myself.

If you decide to collect contact details, do commit to keeping in touch with people regularly by sending newsletters with information of your products, services, incentives and special offers, whilst always directing people to your website.

Try to follow up as quickly as possible as you don't want your potential customers to forget you so I would suggest sending your first introductory email within 24 – 48 hours (See sample email on Form 2 at the back of this book). Keep your emails interesting, short and lighthearted, always selling the benefits of your products. Keep doing this regularly, and you can build loyal customers who will purchase for many months and years plus recommend their friends and family to you.

If you have social media platforms such as Facebook, Instagram or Twitter, do encourage people to like your pages and follow you as these platforms are good promotion and advertising tools. You can also keep people informed of places you will be visiting to sell your work and also any parties or events you will be hosting. By actively building up a following, and communicating with people regularly, you will soon find you can generate sales online in addition to sales at craft fayres.

Do remember to adhere to the rules around data protection, as set out by the UK Government in the Data Protection Act 1998.

If you do not intend to follow up and send emails to people, it's probably best not to collect contact details.

QUESTIONS ?

5.0 Asking the Right Questions

Before booking an event, do consider asking the organiser questions to determine whether it is right for you and your products. Always remember that you are the customer, and entitled to ask questions and explore their service before booking. You are purchasing a service and therefore give it due consideration in the same way you would if you were going to purchase any other product or service.

Below is a series of question and points to consider. Do take time to explore with an organiser before booking an event:

What is the background of the event organiser!

Organising good quality events is a skill. Many professional event organisers undertake years of study to achieve accreditation and qualifications. With the recent boom in craft fayres, some people have spotted opportunities to organise events. Some organisers were once traders themselves and decided to run their own craft fayres, whilst some experienced and professional companies have seen opportunities to get involved.

Do explore the background of the organiser to satisfy yourself that they are sufficiently experienced and/or qualified at organising and managing events that meet your needs. This is especially important if you are paying a significant amount of money to attend.

Bear in mind that event organisers will range from volunteers working for charities or community groups; business owners running event management companies or large corporate management ventures employing teams of professionals.

Do keep your expectations realistic and in proportion. Don't expect to find a professionally qualified event organiser running a small local craft fayres and charging a few pounds. However, it is reasonable to expect a business charging hundreds of pounds at a large event to have a few years of experience and even some qualification.

How many events have they organised, including the particular event you are interested in
Try to establish the track record of the organiser, finding out how many events have they organised in the past. This will open up the way to asking more pertinent questions.

If it's the organiser's first event, then take time to explore their background and the reasons why they have decided to organise events. This can highlight whether they are sufficiently experienced and interested in supporting the crafting community, giving traders a real opportunity to showcase businesses and sell their work.

Advertising & Marketing Methods
Establish what advertising methods the organiser plan to use to promote the event. An experienced organiser will use a variety

of tried and tested methods and should be able to show some evidence of planned activities such as newspaper/magazine articles and adverts, banners up at the venue, posters in shop windows etc.

In the early days, I booked a craft fayre event that was advertised as a weekend craft fayre extravaganza. It was a going to be a two day event in a popular and busy venue located in the heart of the community! Without understanding the need to explore and ask questions, I quickly booked the event after the organiser informed me that space was selling out fast. I spent days preparing for the event and duly got to the venue early to set up.

As I approached the venue, my heart sank. The venue was off the beaten track and there was no visible advertising available such as banners or signs to inform the community of the event.

Whilst I was setting up, I shared my observations with the organiser, who proceeded to inform me not to worry because the venue managers had a database of over 6000 members and they had all been invited. I asked if any other marketing had been done, and was told over 5000 leaflets had been distributed to local homes, businesses, at school gates and a Facebook page created to promote the event. I was nervous and rightly so. Unfortunately only 8 people turned up to the event so it was cancelled at the end of the first morning and all the stall holders were duly part-refunded.

There was a great deal of learning for me from that event, particularly around asking the right questions before booking.

To be fair to organisers, they don't have crystal balls and cannot predict how many people will attend events despite how much hard work and effort they put in. It is in the organiser's interest to get as many customers through the door and to ensure the event is a success – if nothing else, for their reputation and the survival of their business. Therefore, the responsibility is always on the stallholder to do sufficient research to establish if the event is right for them.

An experienced organiser will have an advertising budget and will use a wide variety of paid methods, some of which may include:

- Newspaper and Magazine adverts and articles
- Radio promotions
- Flyers and posters
- Adverts and banners at the venue and surrounding area
- Marketing through existing database of customers and clients
- Working with local businesses

This list is not exhaustive. Satisfy yourself that the advertising methods are sufficient and your customers will attend.

Event Capacity

Establish not only the venue capacity i.e. how many traders the venue can take and how many are expected, but also, and very importantly, how many spaces have been sold.

If the venue hired can hold 60 trader (for example) and a week or so before the event, there is more than about 40% of spaces unsold, explore with the organiser why this is. There could be a wide variety of reasons why spaces have not been sold and this could help you decide whether the event and organiser is right for you.

Experienced organisers of quality and popular event will often sell out of trading spaces quickly and operate a waiting list. Do bear in mind however, that just because an event is popular and a sellout with traders, it doesn't necessarily mean that it is right for you and your products. You still need to explore whether you will meet your customers at that event, i.e. if you are selling items for the Artisan market, think about whether your customers will be at a general craft and gift fayre.

A few years ago, I tried to book a craft fayre. I contacted the organisers who duly informed me of their process (which was via message announcement on their social media page when bookings were open).

I checked every day for about a month to see if their bookings were open. One morning, I checked and discovered the announcement of their bookings being opened had been made. The announcement was made at 9am on the page and at 10.45am, I saw it and rang their offices. I was lucky as they informed I had taken the last space. In less than 2 hours, they had sold out of 120 spaces!

The event had a good reputation amongst traders as it was well organised and there was lots of good quality marketing and advertising that took place in the run up to the event. This resulted in good numbers of customers coming through the door.

Footfall Enquiries

A good organiser should have a range of statistics including number of people that attended their previous events, and on each day (if held over several days). This information is important as it can help you determine whether their events are popular with the public.

If an event has been held previously at a particular venue, then the organiser should have evidence to share with you. Therefore consider asking for:

- Facebook page or Website with details and pictures of any previous events

- Contact details of traders you can approach for a review

- Details of footfall (number of visitors/shoppers) to the event

Do be aware that no matter how good an organiser is, they are not in control of how many people attend and purchase, they can only effectively market and advertise the event and do their best to get as many people as possible in through the door.

Returning Traders

Event organisers with good reputations will attract returning traders. There are not many traders that will repeatedly return to an event if it was not successful for them.

Do enquire from the event organiser the following:

- How many traders are returners?

- Of those return traders, how many events have they previously booked (i.e. 2, 3 or more etc?)

If an organiser has been running events for some time and they have a high turnover of traders, i.e. low number of return traders, then explore the reasons for this.

Be aware that organisers of popular events will have a following of regular traders who book at the same or different venue.

Traders will often return to trade with the same organiser if the show has been good for them, and customer service has been high. Do set your own percentage of what you class is an acceptable figure.

When I ask organisers this question, I like to look for around 65% of traders to be returners. Anything less and I am cautious.

At the event I attended as mentioned in the previous section (Event Capacity), the craft fayre had been running for 6 years and over 80% of traders were returners. The event was so popular with traders that the organiser eventually had to put a system in place to give as many different traders an opportunity to attend and to provide variety for customers.

Before I understood the importance of asking questions of the organiser, I booked to attend a 2 day show. The show had been running for 3 years. Unfortunately the show was not successful for me as there was very little footfall.

When I asked other traders for their experience, everyone I spoke to said it was their first time at the event. I then approached the organiser and sure enough, they confirmed that nearly everyone at the event were new traders. Alarm bell starting ringing and it explained why so many people were new traders. It said to me that previous traders had poor experiences and were not interested in returning.

Location of Craft Fayre

Always take some time to check out the venue before booking. If possible, visit the area and have and look at it with the perspective of the local community. Look at the venue considering whether it will attract good passing trade and if it is visible in the community. Events held off the beaten track that is not easily visible or hard to find can prevent customers attending and therefore limit overall numbers of people attending.

I have made very expensive assumptions booking craft fayres that were held in venues that sounded like it was going to be popular and unfortunately I didn't check it out before booking.

One such event I attended was being held in a Bowling Club on a Bowling night. I booked straight away after making lots of assumptions. I thought it was going to be a ten pin bowling club that was filled with families and held in a leisure/sports arcade. Instead it was an over 60's Bowls Club in a quiet indoor Bowls Centre.

I arrived for the event and was disappointed – the entrance to the venue was via a long dark unlit driveway off the main road. There were no signs or banners on the roadside advertising the event.

My first thoughts as I was driving up the track was that no one is going to walk up from the road, because it was a long walk, on uneven paving with insufficient lighting. The pathway was not disability accessible either. I set up, along with all the other traders and unfortunately it was a very long evening.

Whilst it was bowling night, the bowlers, had not been informed of the craft fayre on site and there were no signs around the building informing them of the event. When I asked why this was, the organisers informed that they were restricted by the club committee with regards to putting up notices around the building.

After waiting 2 hours, and seeing only a handful of people visit the craft fayre, we all packed up and went home. It was a valuable lesson in taking time to check out the venue before booking and not making assumptions.

Is the venue popular with the local Community?
People like to visit popular venues, especially if there will be other attractions going on at the same time. Some of the best craft fayres I have attended have been held in areas where there is other activities happening.

These have been successful because people are going to the location for a family day out and there is lots to see and do. These have included festivals, markets, carnivals and county shows.

I attended on a few occasions a craft fayre that was held in a church with its doors opening up on to a very busy high street. There was a good flow of shoppers coming in throughout the day.

The location of the craft fayre was very important as it felt integrated into the shopping area, plus there was lots of signs and banners inviting people into the venue to shop.

This event was successful for many traders and myself because I believe it was at the heart of the community. During the week it was used for lots of community activities with children, new mums, parents, senior citizens, women's groups and craft groups. There were regular church services throughout the week and at weekends.

Is there good disability access and parking for customers?
Good access is vital not just for traders, but also for visitors. This has often been an important factor in deciding whether to book or not for me. I have been to craft fayres that have poor access (i.e. no lift to get to upper or lower floors) and that has affected the sales of people on different levels as people with mobility

challenges and parents with children in pushchairs cannot easily access these areas.

Also, if a venue has poor parking facilities (i.e. high parking costs or insufficient spaces), this can put customers off attending. If this is the case, do check with the organisers what assistance if any they will provide.

A craft fayre I attended years ago in a listed building had many of these challenges, but the organisers anticipated many of these potential problems and worked hard to overcome them.

The venue was popular in the area, well known and regularly used, making it a great choice, but being a listed building, it had limitations. The organisers had lots of staff available to assist people up and down the stairs and car park staff to direct drivers. These thoughtful touches made the event a success despite the limitations of the venue.

What is included in the price of the Craft Fayre?
This can vary enormously between organisers so do check whether there are any hidden extras to pay such as VAT, parking charges, furniture or electricity. Also check to see if a table and chair will be provided. If a table is provided, check the size. Don't assume it will be a standard 6 x 2ft table.

In the early days, I assumed a table and chair would be standard provisions, only to turn up and find that a table was included, but no chair. I had to stand for the whole day – a very painful experience.

On another occasion, a table was provided, but it was a small 4 x 2ft table, on yet another occasion, the table was a non-standard round table. If I had checked with the organiser beforehand, I would have been able to bring my own suitable table and chair as required.

If you need extra display space, see if you can reserve an extra table, or take one along.

To create interesting displays, I use to take along a set of nest tables and position them at the side and front of my main table. This not only created interest with different levels, but also provided more space for me to display my goods.

I also took along shelving units and placed them on top of my table, allowing me to create not only more height which added interest but also provided much more space. The more products I had out for sale, arranged in an interesting, attractive and eye-catching display, the more opportunities for generating sales.

Wi-Fi

If you need Wi-Fi, to operate your laptop, tablet, phone or card payment machine, do check if this is available and whether there are any charges involved. If events are being held in hotels, town halls and shopping centres, sometimes Wi-Fi usage is chargeable.

Wall Space

If you need wall space to display your work, check whether this is possible. Don't assume wall space will be available or allocated. Some events are held in venues that have large spaces that are divided into sections, sometimes tables are arranged down the centre of the room providing no wall space at all. Also, if exhibiting at County shows, within a marquee, there will be no solid wall space, so consider taking along wall racks if needed.

Loading and Unloading

Check to see what the procedure is for loading and unloading. Some organisers, particularly for large events such as county fayres and events held in exhibition centres operate a system for loading and unloading which can take some time.

You may need to arrive at an allotted time or require passes. Some event organisers may have staff on hand to help you, particularly if you require assistance and ask before the event.

Trader Parking Arrangements

Check to see what the parking arrangements are for stallholders, including where the parking will be, how far away it is and if any permits are needed or any parking fees involved.

I was delighted I asked this question when considering to book a stall at an event. It turned out that the venue had little onsite parking and what arrangements they had was only for blue badge holders. Whilst stallholders were able to use the parking for loading/unloading, it was limited to a few cars only at any given time and a queuing system was operated. The main car park for stallholders and visitors was just over half a mile walk up the road.

Set up and Breakdown Times

Do check set up and breakdown times. Most organisers require all traders to be set up at a specific time before doors open to the public.

Likewise most organisers will require traders to pack down and leave after the show closes, even if it has been a slow day. This is because when traders start packing down and leaving, it does not give a good appearance or provide opportunities for shoppers who are attending the show late in the day, plus it can be hazardous and impact on health and safety for shoppers and other traders.

If the event is being held over 2 or more days, do check if it is safe to leave your stall set up overnight or whether you need to break down and set up again the next day. If you decide to leave your products up overnight, do check with your insurance company beforehand that you are sufficiently covered if products are stolen or damaged. Also handy is to take a covering such as a large table cloth or sheet with which to cover your display.

Promotion Opportunities

Some event organisers may provide an opportunity for traders to advertise and promote their business through either a directory, magazine or show booklet which is provided to visitors or through a link on the main website. This can be valuable for customers who are researching businesses to visit at the event and as a future reference guide.

If you wish to be included in these advertising and promotional opportunities, do check with the event organiser for any associated costs and cut of dates for including your advert and details. Sometimes free advertising space is available, but there may be a financial cost involved. Costs can vary enormously from a few pounds to several hundred for a small space to thousands of pounds for a full page.

If you do wish to consider taking up advertising options, do ensure you have an up to date website with good quality photographs of your work available and carefully review your contact details on all information to be listed to ensure they are current and correct.

As with all advertising opportunities, do think very carefully as there is never any guarantees of gaining business through this method.

BEING

OBJECTIVE...

6.0 Setting Your Objective

It is important to always remember that your objective for attending an event as a trader will be different to the objectives of the organiser. Therefore, if an organiser tells you that they have previously had "good" events, explore what they mean.

Take some time to think about what you want to gain from attending a craft fayre. Things may include:

- Finding local regular events to trade
- Opportunities to meet customers and to get feedback
- Customers ready to purchase your wares
- Affordable events in a popular area
- Good trading spot with easy access
- Good access options for loading and unloading goods
- Good disability access
- Good facilities for parents with children
- Well advertised and promoted
- Friendly and welcoming organiser (and staff on the day)

Use Form 3 at the back of this book to record what you want from each event.

At the end of each event, use Form 4 to review what you learnt and how you can improve on your next event.

Objectives for organisers may include:

- Sell as much space for as much money as reasonably possible
- Keep outgoing costs low to make as much profit possible
- Promote a cause, charity or business
- Get as many shoppers in through the doors. (*No matter how good an organiser is, they have no control over whether customers make purchases or not*).
- Ensure everyone complies with health and safety requirements
- Provide any equipment and sundries as advertised to traders and customers
- Build a list of traders and customers to invite to future events.

This list is not exhaustive and will vary from organiser to organiser.

By contacting an event organiser beforehand, you can explore how closely matched or how far apart your own personal objectives are with theirs, therefore helping you decide whether the event is right for you or not.

As organising and managing events on the day requires full attention, do take some time to ask if the organiser will be trading/selling on the day. It is very difficult for an organiser to look after their customers (traders and visitors) effectively whilst running their own stall. If an organiser will be having a stall, check that they will be having helpers on the day to effectively manage the event, looking after the needs and requirements of everyone. Health and safety is essential and this should be the top priority of the organiser.

GOT IT COVERED!

7.0   Insurances

Do ensure you have sufficient insurance cover in place. You will need as a minimum Public Liability and Product Liability insurance.

Public Liability insurance will be needed to cover the cost of claims made by members of the public for incidents that may occur in connection with your business activities. It may cover legal costs including compensation for any personal injuries, loss of or damage to property.

Product Liability insurance is needed to protect you against any claims of personal injury or property damage caused by any products you have sold or supplied. It is needed to help protect your business by ensuring if in the event of a claim arising, your legal and court costs are covered.

Public and Product Liability is usually sold together as a package by most reputable insurance providers, but do double check this is the case before you purchase your cover.

There are lots of insurances companies available online that can offer insurance. Do explain that you require it for making handcrafted goods and attending craft fayres so they can provide suitable cover to meet your needs.

Whilst lots of insurance companies provide the facility to take out insurance cover online, do contact the company directly and speak to an operator if you have any queries. It is better to do this and know that you have a suitable policy that will cover all your needs than to guess and end up with a policy that does not quite fit your requirements. For example, some insurance policies will not cover jewellery makers that sell earrings – so depending on what you make and offer for sale, do check and ask the question.

Prices do vary enormously for suitable insurance, so shop around. As a guide, insurance should cost between £45 and £100 for a year's worth of cover for general handcrafted items. Some of my clients have contacted me informing they have received quote for £300 plus per annum. This is very expensive and I have recommended shopping around. Some larger event organisers may offer you Public Liability insurance as a convenient option. Do be careful. I was once offered insurance for a 2 day show for £65! This, in my opinion was very hefty, considering my annual insurance costs was only £47.

Another careful consideration is to get as much cover as possible. The more cover does not always mean it will be more expensive. The standard insurance cover in the UK is £1million. A few years ago, I paid £69 per year for £1million of cover, but the following year when I shopped around, I found £5million of cover, plus online insurance for only £47 per year. It really is worth shopping around to get the best deals.

Your event organiser may request to see a copy of your Public Liability Insurance policy for their records and insurance requirements, so do take a copy along to show them in the event this is needed. Some organisers may request a copy of your policy on application or at the time of booking.

Always keep your insurance up to date, checking the expiry date and renewing immediately. I would never recommend doing any craft fayre without valid insurance. Always have it running concurrently as you never know when a claim may arise.

If you are in the UK, do ensure any insurance company you deal with is registered with the Financial Conduct Authority.

CHECK THE CHECKLIST!

8.0   Preparing For Your Craft Fayre

Once you decide on which craft fayres you are going to attend, do think about the practical matters to make the event go as smoothly as possible. You may wish to use Form 5 at the back of this book.

General Items

Products

Take along sufficient items to sell. It is better to take too much than not enough. Only put out enough items to create a good display (not too crowded) and keep spare items out of sight. As items on your table start to sell, you can bring out more stock to replenish your display.

During quiet periods, move the items on your table around. People often walk around a craft fayre a couple of times before leaving. By moving your items around your display, positioning them in different spots, items that didn't catch your customer's eye the first time they walk around can stand out the second time.

I like to take along a duster, particularly when doing outdoor events as over the course of the day, items can get dusty. Keeping them pristine can help achieve the sale as no one wants to buy dusty items.

Packaging Materials

Whatever you decide to package your materials in, do ensure you take plenty along. This may include gift bags, boxes, tissue organza bags etc. Do ensure they are branded or at least have your contact details attached so your customers can find you again in future.

Display Equipment

Take along display equipment to create interesting and eye catching displays that fit with your style of products. For example, if your products have a vintage feel, try incorporating vintage style props into your display using lamps, mirrors, containers, picture frames etc. This creates ambience and interest that can draw customers over.

Portable Lights

Lighting is essential as it will highlight products you want to draw attention to, as well as show all your items off to their best. Whether you are setting up your display inside or outside, consider using either electric lamps or battery operated ones.

If possible, try to use daylight lamps and or light bulbs as it can dramatically enhance your goods rather than standard or tinted light bulbs. Position lights carefully so they are directed on your items and not likely to blind customers. Also useful are fairy lights that that can be weaved in and around your items on the table, creating an eye catching effect.

Electrical Plug Socket Track and Extension Lead

This is will be required for plugging in your electrical lighting. Do talk to your event organiser at the time of booking with regards to whether they will provide electricity. This will determine whether you need to take your track and extension lead along. Some organisers may make a charge for the use of electricity and may have to be requested in advance or offered on a first come basis.

Mirrors

This is essential if selling jewellery, hats, and scarves etc. as customers can see themselves in the items. Do consider having more than one mirror, so customers don't have to wait if one is being used. Do ensure you take a cleaning cloth and polish to keep your mirrors looking pristine at all times.

Table Covering

If your business branding follows a colour theme, then consider incorporating it as part of your table covering, however do be aware that some event organisers may insist on a black or white table covering and may even provide it for you. This will be to give the fayre a uniformed look and may be at the request and requirement of the venue management.

If you can take your own, then do ensure it is big enough to cover the front and sides of your table. Also useful will be safety pins to neatly pin the sides of the tablecloth, creating a trip free zone. Also, create a good impression by ensuring you covering is clean and ironed. For outdoor events, using oilcloth for a table covering enables you to wipe it down, therefore providing clean surfaces compared to using a cotton covering which can gather dust and to is harder to keep clean, especially if your event will be over several days.

PR Material

If you or your work have been featured in magazines, newspapers or on TV, have clippings available for customers to see. It can raise your profile and reputation. Pin these up on a noticeboard and display at the front of your table, or behind you on a wall. Alternatively, put clippings in a picture frame and position in a prominent positon on your table for people to see. Have any items that has been featured, made up ready to sell and when customers stop by, use it as a talking point to create interest in your work.

Marketing Literature

Do ensure you have plenty of flyers, leaflets and promotional materials to give to customers. Ensure your material directs people to your website and includes an irresistible offer.

Your marketing information can be positioned at the front of your table, in easy reach for your customers to access. Also, do keep a few in your hand so when you strike up a conversation with someone, you can easily hand information to them.

Keep your literature clean and tidy at all times, remembering that the presentation of your literature is a reflection of you and your business.

Mailing List & Clip Board

Always take along a mailing list to collect contact details of people you speak to (please see Form 1 at the back of this book). Have plenty of these forms attached to a sturdy clip board so you can easily and quickly take contact details. Also essential will be a working pen. I like to tie a pen to the clipboard, reducing the chance of it going astray. Always ensure you comply with the Data Protection Act 1998 in regards to taking, storing and using personal information.

Business Signage

Branding your stall with your business logo using signs and banners can create a good impression with customers. It can show that you take your business seriously and is also a visual image that will be associated with you and your product that people can remember. There are lots of businesses available online that can create and print suitable branding materials at affordable prices.

Cash Float

Take plenty of change including £1 coins and £5 notes. To minimize the amount of small loose change you need to deal with, do think about rounding up your pricing, i.e. £5 instead of

£4.50; £10 instead of £9 etc. This way, you will be taking notes and need to deal with less change. If you are not comfortable charging £10 instead of £9 for example, then include something additional such as a gift bag.

Decide on a suitable amount for your cash float. I use to have a £30 float made up of 10 x £1; and 4 x £5. This was sufficient for most events.

Receipt Book

Do record all your sales and provide your customers with a receipt (which details your contact information). If the customer does not want a receipt, then still record the sale.

Your receipt book will be invaluable when monitoring sales from all events enabling you to track sales on a monthly, quarterly and annual basis. It will be invaluable for bookkeeping and accounting purposes when submitting your end of year tax returns.

Cash Box or Money Belt

You will need something you can easily and discreetly store your cash in, but also access to deal with change. Some traders like to use a money belt or money apron whilst others like to use a cash box. Whatever you choose to use, ensure you keep your money safe.

Card Payment Machine

Providing customers with an alternative payment method is a good idea. There are options available on the UK market including packages from the Banks and specialist companies. Do consider these options carefully as they can be expensive.

A popular alternative when starting out at craft fayres are portable machines that is linked to a free downloadable phone App on via a smart phone and used with a card reader. These options usually include a one off fee for the card reader and a small fee for any transactions made. A few suggestions include PayPal, Izettle and Payleven. As you will need to use your smart phone and Bluetooth, do ensure you can access Wi-Fi or you have sufficient mobile data available.

Mobile Phone and Charger

If you have a smart phone, they have lots of apps that can be useful when doing craft fayres such as the calculator, memo and money monitor features that can be downloaded for free. If you take your phone along, don't forget to ensure it is fully charged or take your charger along if you know there will be an electricity point available.

Pens/Pencils

Having a pen or pencil is always handy if your customer needs one or you need to jot information down or write out receipts. Always have at least 2, so you have a spare if one doesn't work.

Note Book

Keep this handy to jot down any information that you come across during the fayre. Other traders will often pass on tips and information, so being able to jot them down will save you from having to memorize it.

Price Tags

Take plenty of price tags along and check all your goods are clearly priced. Having extra tags along will be useful in the event that tags fall off your items or become damaged.

Sundry Box

Having a sundry box with various items can come in handy. I always carried with me a little plastic box with a tight fitting lid that has an array of items including scissors, drawing pins, sticky tape, bulldog clips, string, double sided tape, elastic bands, safety pins, bungee cords, painkiller tablets and personal items such as hand cream, lip balm etc. Different craft fayres will have varying set up, in different environments and having a sundry box with bits and pieces can come in really useful.

Table and Chair

Check with the organiser what furniture will be provided or whether you will need to bring your own table and chair. If you need a special chair- i.e. ergonomically designed chair for your back, do take it along.

Depending on space, some organisers may allow an additional small table if you need it. This can be useful either as a packing station or as extra display space.

Public Liability Insurance Policy Schedule

Always have a copy of your policy schedule handy to show your event organiser. Either a paper copy or a digital copy on your phone should suffice.

Personal Comfort

Extra clothing

Taking along a few layers of clothes can be a warm welcome. Even in the summer, a shady or drafty spot where you are set up all day can get chilly and cold so taking extra layers, including cardigan, jacket, scarf, hat, gloves, socks or boots can be a welcomed addition. If you are outdoors in the summer, do think about taking a sun hat, sun lotion and even an umbrella for shade.

Refreshments

Taking along something to eat and drink is sensible, plus it can save you money. If you have to buy refreshments at events, it can start to add up, plus there are no guarantees that refreshment facilities are available or close by, which could mean having to leave your stand for lengthy periods of time whilst you find refreshments.

A bottle of water, a flask of hot tea, coffee or soup and a light meal or sandwiches can keep you going throughout the day. If you have a sweet tooth, a sweet treat can perk you up too.

I have in the past, done events with a few rare organisers who have included refreshments in the cost of the stall fee. Some organisers have offered unlimited supply of hot and cold drinks with biscuits. One event organiser I exhibited with at a county show provided a selection of hot and cold drinks throughout the day plus bacon and egg baps for breakfast and a choice of lunch meals and afternoon snacks including cakes and biscuits. This organiser was very rare. They were a new event management company and offered this great service to their traders to build loyalty.

Blanket

During the cold or damp weather, taking a blanket to keep you warm can be essential, especially if allocated in a drafty spot or outside.

Outdoor Events

Canopy/Mini Marquee

If your event is outdoor, check with the organiser if you need to bring a canopy or mini marquee for your pitch. If you do, check the pitch size and the size of your covering as sometimes organisers may charge if your equipment is outside of your pitch area.

If you need to purchase a canopy or mini marquee, do shop around as prices will vary enormously. Other considerations is to ensure your equipment is waterproof and will keep you and your display dry if it rains. Also think about taking along weights to weigh down the structure as you don't want it blowing away if the weather is windy.

When choosing your canopy or mini marquee, do think about how you will assemble it. Many structures require 2 people for safe assembly. If you are planning to do events on your own, think carefully about whether you will be able to enlist the help of someone to help you for both setting up and breaking down.

Floor Covering

If you will be standing on the hard ground, gravel or grass, do take pieces of carpet or plenty of cardboard to stand on as this can keep your feet warm underfoot.

These are just a few considerations that I have found and there may be some additional ones that are specific to your business.

MONEY MONEY MONEY!

9.0 Cost of Craft Fayres

The cost of craft fayres can vary enormously depending on the type of event you wish to do. These can range from around £10 to £20 for a typical school, church or charity craft fayre event, right through to hundreds and even thousands of pounds for professionally organised events at national venues.

There is no rhyme or reason with Craft Fayres – I have been to small local events and paid £10 for a stall and sold large amounts of products and in comparison, paid hundreds of pounds for well publicized events with high footfall and not recovered my stall cost. Sometimes, I have not covered all the additional let alone all the other costs including travel, accommodation, subsistence, p etc.

On other occasions the reverse has happened – paying £20 for a stall and not having a sale and other times, paying hundreds of pounds and making a good profit.

Do set a budget for how much you want to spend on craft fayres for the year or each month and stick to it. Your budget may also include all additional costs such as travel and accommodation etc. Ensure you can afford all the costs and that these fit within your budget, carefully doing your research as discussed in the earlier pages of this book, weighing up all factors so you are happy with your decision.

BOOK IT...

10.0 Booking Your Craft Fayre

When you are ready to book your event, contact the organiser and check details of how to make the booking. Every event organiser will operate differently. Some require a booking form to be completed, whilst others ask for all interested traders to submit an application and after a closing date, they decide who will be allocated a space. Many traders operate on a first come basis, with a limit on how many traders offer the same type of products, whilst others have no criteria and will take all bookings.

Most organisers require payment at the time of booking, usually by bank transfer or credit card. For large events that costs hundreds or thousands of pounds, organisers may require a deposit and sometimes offer payment plans.

Depending on the size of the craft fayre, you may be able to choose your location.

At County Shows and large craft fayres it is usual for the organiser to send out a floor plan along with booking information. This allows traders to choose which size of stall and position is most suitable along their needs. Each size of stand, and position will often dictate the price, with front, entrance and corner positions being the most visible with customers and therefore being more expensive. The organiser will often indicate all the stalls that are sold and any that are available.

From experience, I learnt that sometimes paying a little extra for a larger size stall that enables you to create an effective and attractive display, and in situated in a prominent position is worthwhile.

In a bid to save money, I booked the smallest size stand available, believing it would be sufficient. I was very disappointed as my space was a tiny 4ft wide and 3ft deep. There was no space to move around and to get in and out, I had to crawl under the table, which was not ideal. My display space was on a 4ft x 2ft table which was much smaller than the standard 6ft table I was use to setting my displays upon. Had I planned more effectively and plotted out the space beforehand, I would not had booked the smallest space, but spent a little extra to get more room and create a good display.

Getting hold of the floor plan, or being able to choose your space beforehand can be essential in planning your display.

Always get a receipt for your payment as this will be needed to keep track of your outgoing expenses and when you do your tax returns. Some organisers, particularly of small local events may not routinely provide a receipt, so do ensure you request one. Most organisers can arrange to send this electronically via email

Do ask for a copy of the terms and conditions and details of any cancellation policy in the event you cannot attend at the last minute. Asking for this before you book and taking time to read through can highlight any potential pitfalls.

If you are booking craft fayres, you may be deemed as running a business by the authorities, so do ensure you are properly registered with HMRC (Her Majesty Revenue and Customs) and you have informed all other authorities as necessary such as the DWP (Department for Works and Pensions) if you are claiming welfare benefits.

CHECK IT OUT!

11.0 Scammers

It is rare, but not uncommon that scammers operate organising craft fayres. By asking questions of the organiser, asking to see evidence of previous events etc. you can satisfy yourself you are dealing with genuine organisers. If someone is pushing you to make payment quickly, be cautious.

I previously came across an organiser who was saying all the right things, but was pushing hard for me to make payment. I will never know if it was genuine, or a scam because I didn't book in the end because I was very wary.

Unfortunately, I have had clients who told me that they were unfortunately scammed. They said the organiser was pushing for payment, so they booked. On the day of the event, they turned up at the venue, along with many other traders, only to find the venue closed and no organiser in sight. They all realized they had been scammed and duly informed the police

.

To avoid scammers, do ask sufficient questions, checking out websites, social media pages, conducting internet searches and where necessary phoning the organiser and speaking to them directly. It is rare, but do always be careful.

IMAGE MATTERS!

12.0 Image Management

When looking for craft fayres, think carefully about what you want your customers to perceive about you and your products and decide whether that can be achieved at each event you wish to do. Be careful never to compromise the image of your business.

For example, if you are offering a quality range of handmade artisan jewellery, beautifully packaged with your usual great style of customer service within a price range of about £100 per piece, think about what your customers would perceive and believe about your products and business if you were to be found at a general gift and craft fayres amongst mass produced imports or low cost handmade items. This could cause confusion in your customers mind, causing them to doubt whether your products were what you say they are. Customers may also see them as overpriced because it is much more expensive than the average item at the show.

By contrast, if your items was at an Artisan fayre where the majority of traders were showcasing their high quality artisan pieces with similar prices, packaging and services as yours, customers would not see your items as out of place, but would see it as a reasonable purchase.

By taking time to think about who your customers are and where you will find them can make a big difference to achieving your sales.

SPEAK & SELL...

13.0 Sell Your Products

There is a common saying that products "sell themselves". If this were true, companies would not invest in training sales people to do their jobs. Products sell when friendly, approachable, knowledgeable and keen people consistently engage people and sell them the benefits of their products.

Ways to do this include:

- Developing a short sales pitch that is friendly, to the point and engaging. Your pitch should be about 10 to 15 seconds in duration. It should succinctly paint a picture of your business, products/service and the benefit it brings to the customers. This short brief introduction should leave the customer wanting to know more, and paves the way for them to ask a question.

- Practicing your rapport and trust building skills, which when done effectively can instill confidence in your customers. It is well known that people buy from people they like and trust. When a customer approaches your stall, you have less than 30 seconds to make a good first impression. Practice how you are going to use this time wisely to make a positive impact.

- Being ready with a positive response to various objections you may receive. Receiving objections is common when selling products, so being ready with a few well thought out responses to common objections can really help you deal with them effectively. A common objective may be that the product is too expensive, in which case a response could be something like "the price reflects the quality and workmanship of the product"

- Making sure you are ready and prepared to take every opportunity that presents itself at craft fayres. If there are only 10 people that visit the event, it means there are 10 opportunities for a sale or to collect contact details! Remember, traders and the organisers can also be your customers too, so don't forget to be ready to offer your products. Also, don't feel obliged to offer a discount just because they are traders or the organiser

- Always being ready to boost your sales by having a show offer and advertising it with clear signs and flyers to make it stand out. Offers can include buy one get a second one half price or 2 for £20 etc. Everyone is looking for a good deal, so having a range that you can discount and offer to your customers can help boost sales.

- Having a range of small affordable items that you can upsell when customers buy a main item. For example, if customers buy a necklace for £40, having a pair of matching earrings that you can sell for a low price such as £5 can increase your takings throughout the day. Alternatively, adding in a matching bracelet and selling the set together, whilst giving the customer suggestions mixing and matching, or gift ideas can increase the sale. If you do this on every sale, your takings can increase significantly over the course of your craft fayre.

Using these tips can help to maximize sales at every craft fayre you attend.

POSITIVITY
CREATES SALES...

14.0 Attitude Matters

Everyone likes a well presented salesperson who knows their products and field of specialism, with a friendly, approachable and warm welcome. Being conscious of your manner, attitude and appearance at all times is important to ensure you are consistent with your overall business image.

For example, if you are presenting your business as a provider of high quality, hand knotted genuine pearl with an average price range of three figures, then ensure your attitude reflects quality. Customers who will part with a lot of money for an item wants the whole experience, not just the product – i.e. they want a warm friendly welcome, attentive service, knowledgeable sales person and confidence of a great after sales service. Your positive attitude towards your potential customers must come across quickly if you are to clinch the sale. This is true for every customer, regardless of the price of an item as £5 for some customers is a lot of money the same way that £500 is for others.

When you have had a long slow and cold day, you may not feel like smiling and being welcoming, but remember, every person at the craft fayre is a potential customer, so ensure you take the opportunity and give every person your best friendly welcome

- *Put yourself in the customer's shoes for a moment and imagine you have been walking around the craft fayre looking for that perfect present for a loved one. It's the end of the day and you are cold, tired and hungry. Your options are to find a gift at the craft fayre or pop into the supermarket on the way home.*

- *You spot a necklace from a distance and walk over to enquire about it. The stallholder is sat behind the table, on their phone and munching on a sandwich. You ask them the price of the necklace and they answer you with a mouthful of food without barely looking up from their phone or getting up out of their seat. You can see they are tired, but you are tired too and is interested in the item.*

- *After stating the price, the stallholder carries on being distracted, not giving you their attention or making any effort to open conversation about the item or showing interest in making the sale. You like the item, the price is right, but their manner is not welcoming. You are undecided what to do. You ask another question and again, get a halfhearted response. Your mind is now made up, the item is overpriced for what it is, the stallholder is unprofessional and the service is poor so you will carry on looking at other stalls on the way out and if you don't find anything suitable, will pop into the supermarket on the way home!*

The sale has been lost because the manner of the stallholder was unprofessional and did not live up to the image of the business.

Some of my best sales have come at the very end of the day, when I felt like packing up and going home. I learnt to always be ready to welcome people, even when I am tired and just want to leave. Sometimes, it's tempting to pack up before the event is finished, especially if the day has not yielded the results you were hoping for, but staying to the end and giving your very best service is always worthwhile.

WORK THE PLAN!

15.0 Planning for Success

To make your next craft fayre successful, take action on the things you have learnt in this book. Take the time to carefully choose your events, asking the right questions and planning carefully.

When my clients put into practice the above principles that I teach, they often go from doing lots of events to just doing a few each year and they get much better results. Remember - It's not the amount of craft fayres you do, but the quality of them that will get you great results.

Once you have carefully considered what you want from attending craft fayres, do ensure you include it in your business plan, recording the types of events you will do and all associated costs.

There are lots of places available where you can access business plans. I would recommend visiting the Jewellery & Crafts Academy website where an easy, useable and practical business plan for creative businesses is available for download.

If you are seeking to make your venture successful, staying on top of all your costs will be essential. Keep a careful eye on all your expenditure, ensuring it is as low as possible so you can make as much money at every opportunity. Record all your financial details in your plan, including not just the cost of the craft fayre, but all additional costs associated with it, including travel, accommodation, packaging, display equipment, parking etc. These costs can mount up, so it is necessary to keep on top of them regularly.

Finally, have fun and celebrate your successes and achievements after each event. Planning, preparing and attending craft fayres can be hard work and it is all part of running a business, therefore it is good to have fun along the way and enjoy it.

16.0 And finally...

I hope you found this book of value and in some small way, I have inspired you, or at least given you a little food for thought.

For more information and all enquiries, please email info@jewellerycraftsacademy.com or visit the website at www.jewellerycraftsacademy.com

Please feel free to visit and join my Facebook Community where you will receive lots of daily inspiration and useful discussions. You can find me at Facebook/The Jewellery & Crafts Academy.

Also please visit the website where there are lots of resources available for download.

I wish you great success in all you do.

Join our Creative Business Community

Visit and like our Facebook page over at

Facebook/The Jewellery & Crafts Academy

Join us for regular inspiration, motivation, news, discussion, support and resources

Also visit our website for the latest blogs, Video trainings, Free EBook, learning resources and downloads at

www.jewellerycraftsacademy.com

Do keep in touch and let me know how you are getting on as we like to offer support, plus share and celebrate successes. Email me at info@jewellerycraftsacademy.com

Forms

Please feel free to copy the following forms
for your personal use only

Form 1

Mailing List

We will keep you up to date with special offers and the latest news. We promise not to spam you and you can unsubscribe from our online newsletter at any time.

Name	Email Address

Form 2

Sample email to send to people who have joined your mailing list

> Dear (*Name*)
>
> Thank you for joining my mailing list. It was a pleasure meeting you at the Craft Fayre at (*Venue*) on (*Date*). I hope you enjoyed the day.
>
> As a "Thank you" for signing up, I would like to offer you (*insert your offer*) when you visit my website and make a purchase.
>
> Please use discount code (*insert your code*). This offer is available until (*insert date*). Please feel free to share this code with your family and friends so they can also benefit from this offer.
>
> (Write a brief summary of who you are and what your business offers. Also ask people to follow your social media pages)
>
> Sign of with your name and Business Name

Suggested Offers Can Include:

- 10% Discount
- Free Postage and Packaging
- Free Gift Packaging
- Buy one get one free
- Buy one get a second one half price
- Buy two, get third half price

Form 3

Craft Fayre Objectives

Date:

Venue:

At this Craft Fayre, my objectives are to:	Outcome
Achieve £................ In sales	
Collect .... contact details by running a prize draw: (i.e. 50 names)	
Meet other traders and exchange ideas	
Find out about other local events	
Gain feedback from customers	
Have fun and enjoy a day out	
Other objectives:	

Form 4

Craft Fayre Review

Date:

Venue:

From this event, I have learnt:

Form 5

Craft Fayre Checklist

In preparation for the Craft Fayre, I will need:

Items	Check
Products	
Packaging	
Display Equipment	
Portable Lights	
Electrical Plug Socket Track and Extension Lead	
Mirrors	
Table Covering	
PR Material	
Marketing Literature	
Mailing List & Clip Board	
Business Signage	
Cash Float	
Receipt Book	
Cash Box or Money Belt	
Card Payment Machine	
Mobile Phone and Charger	
Pens/Pencils	
Note Book	
Price Tags	
Sundry Box	
Table & Chair	
Public Liability Insurance Policy Schedule	

Personal Comfort	
Extra Clothing	
Refreshments	
Blanket	

Outdoor Events	
Canopy/Mini Marquee	
Floor Covering	

Other Items specific to my business	

Jewellery & Crafts
ACADEMY

www.jewellerycraftsacademy.com

Made in the USA
Charleston, SC
29 December 2016